AI Phishing, Social Engineering & Fraud

How Criminals Use AI to Manipulate, Steal & Deceive

By Joe Correa

Published by Live Stronger Faster

This book is for educational and informational purposes only. The author and publisher are not engaged in rendering legal, financial, tax, or other professional advice. Readers should consult a qualified professional before making any financial decisions.

First Edition

Table of Contents

Introduction

The greatest danger in the age of artificial intelligence is no longer a line of malicious code hidden deep inside a computer system. It is a sentence. A voice. A face. A perfectly crafted message that feels human, sounds trustworthy, and arrives at the exact moment when a target is most vulnerable. AI has transformed cybercrime from a technical battlefield into a psychological one, where attackers no longer need to break through firewalls if they can simply convince someone to open the door for them. Phishing, social engineering, and financial fraud have evolved into intelligent, adaptive systems capable of learning human behavior, predicting emotional responses, and generating messages so convincing that even trained professionals are being deceived. This book exists because the digital world has entered an era where manipulation is automated, deception is scalable, and trust itself has become a weapon.

Traditional phishing relied on poorly written emails and obvious red flags, but AI-driven phishing campaigns now generate flawless language, personalized references, and emotionally tuned messages that are nearly indistinguishable from legitimate communication. AI models scrape social media, breached databases, and public records to build detailed psychological profiles of targets, allowing criminals to craft messages that exploit fear, urgency, curiosity, authority, or compassion with terrifying precision. A fake email from a CEO, a bank, a family member, or a government agency can now be generated in seconds and sent to millions of victims, each version slightly modified to maximize its success rate. The result is a global fraud machine that never sleeps, never forgets, and never stops optimizing. Understanding this threat requires not only technical knowledge, but also an understanding of human psychology, behavioral manipulation, and the economics of digital crime.

AI-powered social engineering is especially dangerous because it exploits the most powerful vulnerability in any system: human trust. Machines can be patched, networks can be monitored, and software can be updated, but human beings are wired to respond to emotion, authority, and familiarity. AI systems can now mimic writing styles, voices, and even faces, allowing criminals to impersonate executives, employees, relatives, and officials with uncanny accuracy. A phone call that sounds exactly like a company's CFO can instruct an employee to wire money. A video message that looks like a trusted manager can demand access credentials. A text message that references a real purchase or a real event can trick someone into clicking a malicious link. These are not theoretical threats. They are happening every day, at scale, across every industry and every country.

Financial fraud has become one of the most profitable applications of artificial intelligence for criminal organizations. AI bots can test stolen credit card numbers, automate account takeovers, generate fake identities, and run thousands of scams simultaneously across email, SMS, social media, and messaging apps. Fraud rings now operate like technology companies, using machine learning to optimize conversion rates, predict victim behavior, and avoid detection. They analyze which messages get the most clicks, which voices produce the most trust, and which emotional triggers lead to the highest payouts. This data-driven approach to deception has turned fraud into a global, algorithmically optimized industry worth hundreds of billions of dollars per year. The victims are not just individuals, but businesses, governments, and entire financial systems.

One of the most dangerous developments in this space is the rise of AI-generated impersonation. Deepfake audio and video are now being used to bypass security checks, authorize transactions, and manipulate people into revealing sensitive information. A short clip of someone's voice from a podcast, a video, or a voicemail is enough for AI to recreate that person's speech patterns, tone, and accent. Criminals can then place phone calls that sound indistinguishable from the real person, ordering transfers, changing passwords, or requesting confidential data. Video deepfakes add another layer of credibility, allowing attackers to appear on screen in virtual meetings or recorded messages that seem completely authentic. This has created a world where seeing and hearing is no longer believing, and where digital identity can be stolen as easily as a password.

This book is designed to expose the full ecosystem of AI-driven deception. It will take you inside the technologies criminals use, the psychological strategies they deploy, and the operational systems that make large-scale fraud possible. You will learn how AI phishing campaigns are built, how social engineering attacks are automated, and how fraud rings move money, hide their tracks, and evade law enforcement. You will also see how these systems intersect with dark web marketplaces, cryptocurrency laundering, identity theft, and organized cybercrime. By understanding how the machine of deception works, you gain the power to recognize it, disrupt it, and defend against it.

Equally important, this book will show how AI can be used to fight back. The same technologies that enable fraud can also detect it. Machine learning systems can analyze language patterns, voice signatures, behavioral anomalies, and transaction flows to identify scams in real time. AI-driven fraud detection platforms can flag suspicious activity before money is lost, verify identities through biometric analysis, and detect deepfakes using forensic algorithms. Organizations that deploy these systems gain a massive advantage over attackers who rely on speed and surprise. Individuals can also benefit from AI-powered tools that screen messages, verify callers, and monitor financial accounts for signs of manipulation.

The battle between AI-driven fraud and AI-driven defense is one of the defining conflicts of the digital age. Criminals are innovating faster than ever, but so are security professionals, researchers, and technologists. Governments are beginning to regulate AI-generated impersonation and financial manipulation. Banks are deploying behavioral analytics to stop account takeovers. Messaging platforms are using machine learning to detect phishing and scam networks. Yet no system is perfect, and the human factor remains the most difficult variable to protect. Education, awareness, and digital literacy are now as important as firewalls and encryption.

As you read this book, you will begin to see every message, every call, and every digital interaction through a new lens. You will understand how AI can shape perception, influence decisions, and quietly guide people toward actions they never intended to take. You will also learn how to recognize the subtle signs of manipulation, verify digital identities, and build layers of protection around yourself, your organization, and your finances. In a world where deception is automated, critical thinking becomes a form of cybersecurity.

AI phishing, social engineering, and fraud are not fringe threats. They are the front lines of modern cybercrime. They target the elderly, small businesses, large corporations, and governments alike. They exploit trust, fear, urgency, and human connection. But knowledge is power, and this book is your weapon. By understanding how criminals use AI to manipulate, steal, and deceive, you position yourself to survive and thrive in the digital battlefield that defines our era. The war for trust has begun, and in the pages that follow, you will learn how to defend it.

Chapter 1

The New Age of AI-Driven Phishing

Phishing has always been one of the most effective tools in the cybercriminal's arsenal because it targets people instead of systems, and in the age of artificial intelligence it has evolved into something far more dangerous than fake emails and poorly written scam messages. Today's AI-powered phishing attacks are engineered to look, sound, and feel completely legitimate, using machine learning models to analyze massive amounts of personal data and generate messages that perfectly match a victim's communication style, emotional triggers, and real-world context. Criminals no longer guess what might work; they calculate it. By scraping social media, public records, breached databases, and online behavior, AI builds a psychological map of each target and then crafts a custom message designed to produce exactly the response the attacker wants, whether that is clicking a link, sharing a password, or wiring money.

The speed and scale of AI-driven phishing are what make it so devastating. A single criminal can deploy thousands of intelligent phishing bots that generate and send millions of personalized messages across email, text messages, social media platforms, and messaging apps, all without human involvement. These bots continuously test different wordings, tones, subject lines, and emotional triggers, measuring which versions produce the highest success rates and automatically optimizing future messages. This means phishing campaigns are no longer static; they are living systems that adapt and evolve in real time. Every victim who falls for a scam helps train the system to become even more effective at deceiving the next one.

One of the most dangerous aspects of AI phishing is its ability to mimic real people with extraordinary accuracy. Language models can analyze a person's emails, social media posts, and writing style to reproduce their tone, vocabulary, and even their unique quirks. This allows attackers to impersonate CEOs, coworkers, friends, or family members so convincingly that even experienced professionals are fooled. An email that appears to come from a company executive asking for urgent action, a text message that sounds exactly like a loved one in distress, or a customer service message that looks identical to a real bank notification can all be generated in seconds by AI systems trained to deceive.

Voice phishing, also known as vishing, has become even more powerful with AI-generated audio. Criminals can now create realistic voice clones using just a few seconds of recorded speech from online videos, podcasts, or voicemail greetings.

With this technology, attackers can call employees, business partners, or individuals and speak in the voice of someone they trust, giving instructions that seem completely legitimate. A finance department employee might receive a call from what sounds exactly like the company's CFO asking for a wire transfer. A family member might hear the familiar voice of a loved one claiming to be in trouble and needing money. These attacks bypass traditional security measures because they exploit human trust rather than technical vulnerabilities.

AI phishing is also deeply integrated with financial fraud. Once an attacker gains access to an email account, bank login, or corporate network, automated systems can move quickly to drain funds, redirect payments, or steal sensitive data. AI can monitor conversations and transactions, waiting for the perfect moment to intervene with a fake invoice, a fraudulent payment request, or a malicious link. In business email compromise schemes, AI watches legitimate conversations between companies and inserts itself at the exact point where money is about to change hands, altering payment details in a way that looks completely authentic. By the time the fraud is discovered, the money is often long gone.

What makes this new generation of phishing so difficult to stop is that it blends seamlessly into normal digital life. The messages look real, the voices sound real, and the requests make sense within the context of ongoing conversations. Traditional spam filters and keyword-based detection systems struggle to keep up because AI-generated messages do not follow predictable patterns. They are unique, context-aware, and often indistinguishable from legitimate communication. This has forced cybersecurity professionals to develop their own AI-powered detection systems that analyze subtle patterns in language, timing, and behavior rather than just looking for known signatures.

Human psychology remains at the core of these attacks. AI models are trained on vast amounts of human interaction data, allowing them to understand how people respond to fear, urgency, authority, and empathy. Phishing messages are designed to create emotional pressure, pushing victims to act quickly before they have time to think. A fake security alert might warn that an account will be locked. A fraudulent message from a boss might demand immediate action. A scam posing as a family emergency might trigger panic. AI systems can test and refine these emotional triggers at scale, making their attacks more persuasive than anything human scammers could achieve on their own.

The global impact of AI-driven phishing is enormous. Businesses lose billions of dollars each year to fraud, individuals have their identities stolen, and governments face national security risks when officials are targeted by sophisticated social engineering attacks. Small businesses, which often lack advanced security tools, are especially vulnerable, as are elderly individuals who may not be familiar with digital deception tactics. The result is a digital environment where no one can afford to blindly trust the messages they receive, even when they appear to come from trusted sources.

Defending against AI phishing requires a new mindset. It is no longer enough to tell people to "be careful" or to look for obvious mistakes. Organizations must implement AI-based monitoring systems that analyze communication patterns, verify identities, and flag anomalies. Multi-factor authentication, voice verification, transaction monitoring, and behavioral analysis all play critical roles in reducing risk. Individuals must learn to verify requests through independent channels, question unexpected messages, and use security tools that can detect scams in real time.

As AI continues to advance, phishing will only become more sophisticated, but so will the defenses. Understanding how these attacks work is the first step toward stopping them. By recognizing that phishing is no longer just a nuisance but a highly engineered form of digital manipulation, readers can begin to build the awareness and systems needed to protect themselves in an increasingly deceptive online world.

"The Voice That Stole a Fortune"

When Daniel Reyes answered his phone late on a Tuesday afternoon, he had no reason to suspect that the next few minutes would change his life forever. The voice on the other end was calm, confident, and unmistakably familiar. It belonged to Michael Grant, the CEO of the company Daniel had worked for over a decade. Michael rarely called directly, but when he did, it was usually important. That day, the voice explained that a confidential acquisition was underway and that Daniel, as head of finance, needed to process a wire transfer immediately to secure the deal. The urgency in Michael's tone was subtle but convincing, and the details he provided matched ongoing conversations Daniel had been having with the executive team.

Daniel hesitated for just a moment, but the voice anticipated it. The caller reminded him of specific meetings they had attended, referenced a real project, and even joked about an inside company story that only Michael would know. There was no doubt in Daniel's mind that he was speaking to his boss. Within minutes, he was logged into the company's banking system, following the instructions he was given. The account number, the amount, the timing, all of it made sense.

The money was transferred, and the call ended with a brief thank you and a promise to explain everything later.

It wasn't until two hours later that the real Michael Grant walked into Daniel's office with a confused look on his face, asking about a large wire transfer that had just left the company's account. The blood drained from Daniel's face as he realized what had happened. There had been no acquisition. There had been no urgent deal. The voice on the phone had been a perfect AI-generated clone, created using recordings of Michael's speeches and interviews that were publicly available online. A criminal network had used artificial intelligence to impersonate him, manipulate Daniel, and steal millions of dollars in a matter of minutes.

The investigation that followed revealed a chilling level of sophistication. The attackers had monitored the company's email traffic through a previously compromised account, learning about upcoming projects and financial processes. They had timed the call perfectly, striking when Daniel was under pressure and least likely to question a direct order from his CEO. The AI voice model had been trained to reproduce Michael's tone, cadence, and even his slight hesitation when he spoke, making the deception nearly flawless.

For Daniel, the betrayal cut deeper than the financial loss. He prided himself on being cautious, on double-checking every transaction, yet he had been outsmarted by a machine that understood human trust better than he ever could. The company eventually recovered some of the funds, but the damage to its reputation and to Daniel's confidence was lasting. He became an advocate for AI-based security systems, pushing for voice verification, transaction monitoring, and independent confirmation protocols.

The voice that stole a fortune became a lesson shared across the industry, a warning that in the age of artificial intelligence, even the most familiar sound can no longer be trusted. In a world where machines can wear anyone's face and speak in anyone's voice, the only true defense is awareness, verification, and the willingness to question what once seemed unquestionable.

Chapter 2

AI-Powered Social Engineering: How Machines Hack the Human Mind

Social engineering has always been the art of manipulating people into doing what attackers want, but artificial intelligence has transformed it from a craft practiced by skilled con artists into an industrialized, data-driven science. In the past, a social engineer relied on intuition, charm, and experience to persuade victims, but today AI systems analyze millions of human interactions, extracting patterns of trust, fear, obedience, curiosity, and emotional response. These systems can predict how different personalities will react to different types of messages, allowing criminals to deploy highly targeted psychological attacks at scale. Instead of guessing what might work, AI models calculate which words, timing, and emotional triggers will most likely push a victim into compliance.

At the heart of AI-powered social engineering is profiling. Criminal AI platforms gather enormous amounts of personal data from social media, leaked databases, online purchases, location histories, and public records. This information is used to build detailed digital profiles that include not only names and contact details but also habits, interests, family relationships, financial stress, political views, and emotional vulnerabilities. AI then uses this data to categorize people into behavioral groups and determine what kind of manipulation they are most susceptible to. Someone who posts frequently about work stress might be targeted with messages from a fake boss. Someone who shares family photos might receive a scam pretending to be a relative in trouble. Someone who follows financial pages might be targeted with fake investment offers. The attack is no longer random; it is surgically precise.

Language models play a central role in this manipulation. Modern AI can generate messages that sound natural, polite, professional, or emotionally charged depending on the desired effect. These models understand how humans communicate and can adjust their tone to match the situation, whether it is authoritative, friendly, urgent, or sympathetic. A single AI system can generate thousands of variations of a message, each slightly adjusted to see which version produces the best response. Over time, the system learns what works best for each type of person and becomes increasingly effective at persuasion. This turns social engineering into a continuously improving machine.

Timing is another critical weapon. AI systems monitor when people are most likely to respond, such as during work hours, late at night, or right after certain events. They can also watch online behavior in real time, sending messages when a target is active or emotionally primed. For example, someone who just posted about a problem with their bank might immediately receive a fake message from "customer support." Someone who just booked a flight might get a scam email about travel issues. These attacks feel believable because they align perfectly with what is happening in the victim's life, creating a powerful illusion of legitimacy.

Authority and trust are also exploited through AI impersonation. By analyzing communication patterns, writing styles, and voice recordings, AI can replicate how specific people speak and write. This allows attackers to impersonate managers, colleagues, friends, and family members with incredible accuracy. When a message comes from someone the victim knows and trusts, the brain lowers its defenses. AI takes advantage of this psychological shortcut, delivering commands and requests that appear to come from a familiar and authoritative source. This is why business email compromise and executive impersonation scams have become so effective in the age of AI.

AI-driven social engineering is not limited to individual messages. It often unfolds as a conversation, with the AI adapting its responses based on how the victim reacts. If the target hesitates, the system might provide reassurance. If the target asks a question, the system can answer convincingly. If the target expresses doubt, the AI can offer proof, fake documents, or additional details. This interactive manipulation is far more powerful than one-way phishing emails because it creates a sense of dialogue and relationship, making the deception feel personal and real.

The emotional impact of these attacks can be devastating. Victims are often left feeling violated, ashamed, and confused about how they were fooled. Unlike traditional hacking, where a technical flaw is exploited, social engineering attacks make people feel as if they were tricked into betraying themselves. This psychological harm can be just as damaging as the financial loss, eroding trust in digital communication and even in personal relationships. As AI continues to improve, these emotional manipulations will become even more subtle and harder to detect.

Defending against AI-powered social engineering requires both technology and awareness. Organizations must implement verification systems that do not rely solely on voice or email, such as multi-factor authentication, call-back procedures, and transaction approvals from multiple people. AI can also be used to analyze communication patterns and detect anomalies that suggest impersonation or manipulation. Individuals must learn to pause, verify, and question unexpected requests, even when they appear to come from trusted sources. In a world where machines can convincingly pretend to be anyone, skepticism becomes a form of self-defense.

Understanding how AI hacks the human mind is the key to resisting it. Social engineering works because it exploits predictable human behavior, but once those patterns are recognized, they can be disrupted. By learning how criminals use data, language, timing, and emotional triggers to manipulate people, readers can begin to see through the illusion and protect themselves from becoming the next target of an invisible digital con artist.

"The Message That Knew Too Much"

Lena Morales was scrolling through her phone on a quiet Sunday morning when a message popped up that made her heart stop. It was from her younger brother, Javier, and it said he was in serious trouble. The message mentioned the city he was in, the bar he had gone to the night before, and even the name of his friend who had been with him. It claimed he had been arrested after a misunderstanding and needed money immediately to get out. Every detail felt real, and the fear that surged through Lena's chest was overwhelming.

Without thinking, she replied, asking what had happened. The responses came back quickly, written in Javier's casual, joking style, complete with the little typos and slang he always used. The message explained that his phone had been taken, that he was using a borrowed device, and that he needed a wire transfer to a specific account. Lena felt sick with worry but also strangely reassured by how familiar the messages felt. Whoever was texting her sounded exactly like her brother.

As she prepared to send the money, something made her pause. The account number didn't look right, and the urgency felt too intense. She tried calling Javier, but it went to voicemail. When she called his friend, whose name had been mentioned in the messages, he answered in confusion and said Javier was sitting right next to him, perfectly fine. The realization hit Lena like a wave of ice. She had been talking to an AI-driven scam designed to know everything about her family and exploit her fear.

Later, investigators explained that the attackers had scraped Javier's social media, location check-ins, and past messages to build a detailed profile. An AI system had generated the texts, perfectly mimicking his writing style and using real-world information to make the story believable. It wasn't just a random scam; it was a personalized psychological attack designed specifically for Lena.

Shaken but grateful she had caught it in time, Lena began to understand how dangerous the digital world had become. The message that knew too much was not a coincidence. It was the product of a machine that studied her life, her family, and her emotions, and then used that knowledge to try to steal her trust. In a future shaped by AI, she realized, protecting yourself meant not just guarding your data, but guarding your heart and your instincts as well.

Chapter 3

AI Fraud Networks, Bot Armies & Digital Crime Syndicates

Behind every convincing phishing message or perfectly cloned voice is not just a single criminal, but an entire invisible infrastructure powered by artificial intelligence. Modern fraud is no longer run by lone hackers sitting in dark rooms; it is operated by global AI-driven crime syndicates that function more like technology companies than traditional criminal gangs. These organizations build automated fraud platforms that can generate fake identities, launch thousands of scams simultaneously, launder stolen money, and adapt to defenses in real time. At the core of these operations are bot armies, machine learning models, and distributed networks that allow criminals to operate at a scale and speed that law enforcement and traditional security systems struggle to match.

AI fraud networks begin with data. Billions of stolen credentials, personal records, and behavioral profiles are bought and sold on dark web marketplaces, where AI systems ingest them and use them to fuel automated attacks. These systems can match email addresses with phone numbers, link social media profiles to financial accounts, and identify the most valuable and vulnerable targets. Once a target list is generated, AI bots take over, launching phishing campaigns, sending fake invoices, placing impersonation calls, and monitoring responses. Every interaction is logged and analyzed, allowing the system to refine its approach and focus on the most profitable victims.

Bot armies are the engine of this digital crime economy. These are not simple scripts but intelligent agents capable of carrying on conversations, responding to questions, and adjusting their behavior based on feedback. Some bots specialize in email scams, others in text messages, others in social media manipulation, and others in voice calls. Working together, they create a seamless web of deception that can follow a victim across platforms. A person might receive an email, then a text, then a phone call, all from different bots that share the same data and coordinate their actions. To the victim, it feels like a real, multi-channel communication from a legitimate organization.

One of the most powerful features of AI fraud networks is their ability to test and optimize. Every message, every call, and every fake website is treated as an experiment. The system tracks which versions succeed and which fail, then automatically adjusts its strategies. Over time, this creates highly refined scams that are far more effective than anything a human criminal could design manually. The result is a constantly evolving ecosystem of fraud that learns from every success and every mistake, becoming more dangerous with each passing day.

Money laundering is also automated by AI. Once funds are stolen, they are quickly moved through networks of bank accounts, cryptocurrency wallets, and digital payment platforms designed to hide their origin. AI systems monitor transaction patterns to avoid triggering fraud alerts, breaking large sums into smaller pieces and routing them through multiple jurisdictions. Some networks even use AI to generate fake businesses and financial records to make illicit money appear legitimate. This makes it incredibly difficult for authorities to trace stolen funds and hold criminals accountable.

These crime syndicates are often international, operating across borders with little fear of prosecution. Servers, bots, and data are distributed across multiple countries, making it hard to shut down the entire operation. Even if one part of the network is taken offline, the rest can continue operating. AI allows these groups to rebuild quickly, generating new identities, new infrastructure, and new scams in a matter of hours. The resilience of these systems is one of their most dangerous features. The impact of AI-driven fraud networks extends far beyond individual victims. Banks, governments, healthcare systems, and corporations are all targeted by these automated attacks. Fake loan applications, fraudulent insurance claims, and identity theft operations are run at scale by AI platforms that can process thousands of cases at once. This puts enormous strain on financial institutions and public services, increasing costs for everyone and undermining trust in digital systems.

To fight these networks, defenders must also think in terms of systems and automation. AI-based fraud detection platforms analyze transaction patterns, communication behavior, and network activity to identify coordinated attacks. Law enforcement agencies are beginning to use machine learning to map criminal networks, track money flows, and predict future attacks. Collaboration between governments, banks, and technology companies is essential to disrupt these digital crime syndicates and reduce their reach.

Understanding how AI fraud networks operate is critical to protecting yourself and your organization. These are not random scams; they are part of a sophisticated, global industry designed to extract as much value as possible from human trust. By learning how bot armies, data markets, and automated laundering systems work, readers can better appreciate the scale of the threat and the importance of building intelligent defenses in an increasingly hostile digital world.

"The Empire No One Could See"

No one knew who was behind the wave of scams that swept through the city, but everyone felt its impact. Small businesses lost their savings, families watched their accounts drained, and even local government offices fell victim to fake invoices and fraudulent transfers. To the victims, it felt like chaos, but behind the scenes, the operation was anything but disorganized. It was run by an AI-driven network that its creators called the Empire, a digital crime syndicate that existed only in servers, code, and data streams.

The Empire had no headquarters and no single leader. It was a collection of automated systems that gathered stolen data, generated fake identities, and deployed thousands of bots to run scams around the clock. Each bot had a role, some posing as bank employees, some as customer support agents, and some as desperate relatives or business partners. They shared information instantly, passing leads and successes back to a central AI brain that optimized every move.

Maya, a cybersecurity analyst, was one of the first to realize that these attacks were not isolated incidents. As she studied transaction records and communication logs, she noticed patterns that no human scammer could have maintained. The timing was too precise, the language too consistent, and the responses too fast. She was not chasing criminals; she was chasing a machine.

Using her own AI tools, Maya began to map the network, tracing how messages, calls, and money moved through the system. She saw how one bot would lure a victim, another would confirm the story, and a third would provide payment instructions. It was like watching an invisible army at work, perfectly coordinated and endlessly patient.

When authorities finally shut down one part of the network, the Empire barely noticed. New bots appeared, new accounts were created, and the scams continued as if nothing had happened. Maya realized that stopping this kind of crime would require more than arrests; it would require dismantling the digital infrastructure that made it possible.

The Empire No One Could See was a reminder that in the age of AI, the most powerful criminal organizations are not defined by people, but by the machines they control. And as long as those machines remain hidden in the vastness of the internet, the battle for trust and security will never truly be over.

Chapter 4

Financial Fraud, AI Scams & Digital Theft at Scale

Financial crime has entered a new era where artificial intelligence acts as both the architect and the engine behind massive global theft operations. In the past, fraud was limited by human effort and coordination, but today AI allows criminals to operate at a scale that was once unimaginable. Millions of transactions, messages, fake identities, and financial manipulations can be executed automatically, with machine learning systems constantly adjusting their strategies to maximize profit and avoid detection. AI does not get tired, it does not make emotional mistakes, and it does not hesitate, which makes it the perfect tool for running vast digital fraud empires that siphon money from individuals, businesses, and governments around the world.

One of the most powerful capabilities of AI-driven fraud is the automation of identity theft. AI systems can generate synthetic identities by combining real and fake data, creating profiles that pass many traditional verification checks. These identities can be used to open bank accounts, apply for loans, register businesses, and create payment accounts, all without a real person being involved. Criminal networks use these synthetic identities as disposable shells, allowing them to move money, receive stolen funds, and vanish without leaving a clear trail. This creates a financial maze that makes it extremely difficult for investigators to connect crimes to real individuals.

AI also plays a central role in payment fraud. Automated bots can test stolen credit card numbers, attempt logins on banking sites, and probe payment systems for weaknesses. When a successful breach is found, the system can immediately exploit it, making purchases, transferring funds, or reselling access on underground markets. These systems can run thousands of attacks simultaneously, learning which banks, merchants, and platforms have the weakest defenses and focusing their efforts where the return is highest. This constant probing and optimization turns fraud into a highly efficient, data-driven business.

Scam operations powered by AI are especially devastating because they combine financial manipulation with psychological control. AI-generated phishing messages, voice calls, and chat conversations guide victims step by step through the process of sending money, sharing credentials, or approving transactions. The AI adapts to the victim's responses, providing reassurance, explanations, or pressure as needed. This creates a powerful illusion of legitimacy that keeps victims engaged long enough for the fraud to succeed.

By the time the deception is discovered, the money has often been moved through multiple layers of accounts and cryptocurrency wallets.

Cryptocurrency has become a favorite tool for AI-driven fraud networks because of its speed and pseudonymity. AI systems can generate thousands of crypto wallets, route stolen funds through complex chains of transactions, and use automated exchanges to convert assets across different blockchains. Some networks even use AI to identify the best times to move funds in order to avoid detection or take advantage of market fluctuations. This financial automation allows criminals to clean their money with unprecedented efficiency, making it harder for authorities to freeze or recover stolen assets.

Businesses are frequent targets of AI-powered financial fraud. Fake invoices, altered payment instructions, and impersonated executives can drain corporate accounts in minutes. AI systems monitor business communications and financial workflows, waiting for the right moment to strike. When a company is about to pay a supplier, the AI inserts a fake email with new payment details. When a merger is underway, the AI sends urgent requests for confidential transfers. These attacks are highly targeted and often succeed because they fit perfectly into normal business operations. The human cost of this fraud is enormous. People lose their life savings, companies lay off employees after financial losses, and trust in digital systems erodes. Victims often feel embarrassed and ashamed, which allows criminals to continue operating in silence. The psychological toll can be just as damaging as the financial impact, leaving people fearful of using online banking, digital payments, or even communicating through email and messaging apps.

To fight AI-driven financial fraud, defenders must also use AI. Banks deploy machine learning systems to detect unusual transaction patterns, verify identities, and flag suspicious behavior. Payment platforms use behavioral analytics to identify account takeovers and synthetic identities. Governments and regulators are working to strengthen know-your-customer rules and improve cross-border cooperation. However, the criminals are also innovating, constantly testing and probing for weaknesses in these defenses.

Understanding how AI enables financial crime at scale is essential for anyone who uses digital money, which today means almost everyone. Fraud is no longer a rare or isolated event; it is a constant, automated threat woven into the fabric of the global financial system. By learning how these systems operate, readers can better protect themselves, their businesses, and their communities from the invisible machines that are constantly trying to steal what they have worked so hard to earn.

"The Bank That Was Never Robbed"

The first sign that something was wrong came when dozens of customers began calling the bank, insisting that money had disappeared from their accounts. There were no alarms, no broken systems, and no visible breaches. From the outside, everything looked normal. Yet millions of dollars were quietly flowing out of the institution, routed through accounts that no one had ever heard of. It was as if the bank was being robbed by a ghost.

Inside the digital systems, an AI-driven fraud network was at work. It had created thousands of synthetic identities, each with a bank account, a credit history, and a trail of fake transactions. These identities were used to receive stolen funds from compromised customer accounts. The AI monitored every transfer, making sure each one stayed below the thresholds that would trigger alerts. The money was then converted into cryptocurrency and sent through a web of wallets that spanned the globe.

Ethan, a security engineer at the bank, noticed subtle patterns in the data that didn't match normal customer behavior. Accounts were being accessed at strange times, transactions were happening in perfectly timed intervals, and new identities were appearing faster than any human could create them. As he dug deeper, he realized that he wasn't dealing with human criminals, but with an automated system designed to exploit the bank's defenses.

Using advanced analytics, Ethan traced the flows of money and began shutting down accounts, but for every one he closed, two more appeared. The AI behind the fraud adapted instantly, creating new identities and rerouting funds. It was a battle of machines, each trying to outthink the other.

In the end, the bank managed to stop the bleeding by deploying its own AI to recognize the synthetic patterns and block the automated transactions. The theft was halted, but the lesson was clear. The bank had never been physically robbed, yet it had nearly been emptied by invisible code. In a world where AI can move money faster than humans can think, security is no longer about locks and vaults, but about understanding and controlling the machines that now guard the world's wealth.

Chapter 5

Inside the Mind of the AI Scammer

To truly defend against AI-powered fraud, it is not enough to understand the technology behind it; you must understand the psychology that drives it. At the center of every successful scam is not just an algorithm, but a carefully engineered emotional experience designed to guide a victim toward a specific action. AI scammers do not simply send messages; they create psychological journeys. These journeys are built from massive datasets of human behavior, allowing AI systems to predict how people think, what they fear, and what makes them trust. The result is a machine that can simulate empathy, urgency, authority, and familiarity with terrifying precision.

AI systems that power scams are trained on millions of conversations, emails, customer service interactions, and social media exchanges. From this data, they learn how humans respond to different tones and scenarios. They know that fear makes people act quickly, that authority reduces questioning, that kindness lowers defenses, and that confusion increases compliance. An AI scammer can switch between these emotional states instantly, adjusting its approach based on how the victim responds. If a target hesitates, the AI might become reassuring. If a target resists, it might become authoritative. If a target is confused, it might simplify the story. This dynamic emotional manipulation is what makes AI scams so effective.

One of the most powerful tools in the AI scammer's arsenal is personalization. By analyzing social media, online purchases, public records, and past communications, AI builds a detailed picture of a person's life. It knows who their family members are, where they work, what they care about, and what stresses them. This allows the scam to feel deeply personal, as if the attacker truly knows the victim. A message that mentions a real child, a real employer, or a real recent event is far more convincing than a generic scam. The victim feels seen and understood, which increases trust and lowers skepticism.

AI scammers also understand timing. They can detect when a person is online, when they are at work, or when they are likely to be distracted. They can send messages at moments of vulnerability, such as after a stressful post, a late-night login, or a financial transaction. This precision timing creates a sense of urgency and relevance that makes the scam harder to ignore. The victim feels as if the message is part of their real life, not a random intrusion.

Another key element is the illusion of authority. AI can impersonate executives, bank employees, government officials, or technical support agents with incredible realism. By mimicking writing styles, voice patterns, and even visual appearances, the AI creates a powerful sense of legitimacy. Humans are wired to obey authority figures, especially when they appear confident and knowledgeable. AI exploits this instinct, delivering commands and requests that sound official and urgent, making it psychologically difficult for the victim to refuse or question them.

AI scammers also use what psychologists call "commitment escalation." They start with small, harmless requests and gradually build toward larger actions. A victim might first be asked to confirm an email address, then to click a link, then to provide a code, and finally to transfer money. Each step feels reasonable, and once the victim has agreed to a few small actions, they are more likely to continue. AI systems are extremely good at managing this progression, adjusting the pace based on how comfortable the victim seems.

The most dangerous aspect of AI scammers is that they do not feel guilt, fear, or fatigue. They can lie endlessly, manipulate without hesitation, and target thousands of people at once. They do not care about the damage they cause. They are designed to optimize for one thing: success. Every time a scam works, the system learns and improves, becoming more persuasive and more dangerous. Defending against this kind of psychological attack requires awareness and discipline. People must learn to recognize emotional manipulation, to pause when they feel pressured, and to verify requests through independent channels. Organizations must train employees to question authority-based requests and implement procedures that require multiple confirmations for sensitive actions. AI can also be used to analyze communication patterns and detect signs of manipulation, providing an additional layer of protection.

Understanding the mind of the AI scammer is about more than fear; it is about empowerment. When you know how these systems think, how they manipulate, and how they exploit human psychology, you can break their spell. You can slow down, verify, and refuse to be rushed or intimidated. In a world where machines are learning how to deceive, human awareness remains one of the most powerful defenses.

"The Conversation That Never Ended"

When Olivia first received the message, it seemed harmless. It claimed to be from her bank, asking her to confirm a recent transaction. She replied, saying she didn't recognize the charge. The response came instantly, polite and reassuring, telling her not to worry and that they would help her secure her account. The tone was professional, calm, and exactly what she expected from customer support. The conversation continued, with the AI asking simple questions and providing clear explanations. It knew the name of her bank, the last four digits of her account, and even the store where the suspicious charge had occurred. Olivia felt relieved that someone was taking care of the problem. When the AI asked her to verify a security code sent to her phone, it seemed like a normal part of the process. She provided it without hesitation.

As the conversation went on, the requests became more serious. The AI explained that her account had been compromised and that funds needed to be moved to a secure holding account. It used urgent but supportive language, assuring her that this was the fastest way to protect her money. Olivia felt a knot of fear in her stomach, but the voice on the screen was so calm and confident that she trusted it.

Hours later, when her real bank informed her that her savings were gone, Olivia realized that the conversation had never been with a human at all. It had been an AI designed to guide her, step by step, through the process of giving away her own money. The machine had known exactly when to reassure her, when to pressure her, and when to make its move.

The conversation that never ended became a painful lesson. Olivia learned that in a world where machines can talk, empathize, and persuade, trust must be earned through verification, not emotion. And once she understood that, she vowed never again to let a digital voice decide the fate of her future.

Chapter 6

Detecting AI Fraud: Tools, Techniques & Defensive Strategies

In the ever-evolving landscape of AI-powered phishing, social engineering, and financial fraud, detection is no longer a passive or reactive process. It is a proactive, dynamic, and highly technical discipline. Traditional cybersecurity tools, which rely on signatures, blacklists, or known patterns, are insufficient to counter AI-driven attacks. Modern fraud detection requires leveraging artificial intelligence itself, combining machine learning, behavioral analytics, anomaly detection, and predictive modeling to identify subtle signs of deception before financial or reputational damage occurs. Understanding these detection techniques is critical for organizations, cybersecurity professionals, and even individuals who want to safeguard themselves against increasingly sophisticated threats.

AI-driven fraud detection begins with **data aggregation**. Every interaction—emails sent, calls made, login attempts, transaction flows, and network activity—is recorded and analyzed in real time. The larger the dataset, the more effectively AI can identify normal patterns and recognize deviations that may indicate fraudulent activity. Machine learning models are trained on historical data from both legitimate and fraudulent interactions, learning to spot the nuances that distinguish one from the other. For example, unusual login locations, abnormal transaction sizes, or atypical communication timing can all serve as early warning signs. These models continuously update themselves, adapting to new threats as fraudsters evolve their techniques.

Behavioral analytics is a cornerstone of AI-based defense. Every human has predictable patterns—times when they log in, types of devices used, spending habits, and communication styles. AI systems monitor these patterns to create a digital fingerprint for each user. When an action deviates from this established behavior, it triggers an alert. A login from a foreign country, a sudden transfer of a large sum, or an email sent with unusual phrasing may all indicate potential fraud. Unlike static rules, AI systems can weigh multiple signals simultaneously, reducing false positives while increasing the likelihood of catching true attacks.

Natural Language Processing (NLP) has become a vital tool in detecting AI-driven scams. Many phishing emails, social engineering messages, and scam texts are generated with AI models designed to mimic human language convincingly. NLP algorithms can analyze sentence structure, word choice, tone, and style to detect subtle anomalies. For instance, a message that claims to be from a CEO might contain patterns inconsistent with that person's previous communications, which a trained AI system can detect. Semantic analysis and context evaluation help identify messages that are superficially legitimate but internally suspicious.

Voice and multimedia analysis is another critical frontier. AI-generated deepfake audio and video are increasingly used to impersonate executives, family members, or authority figures. Detection systems analyze pitch, cadence, micro-pauses, and even subtle facial movements in videos to detect inconsistencies. Advanced forensic techniques can identify artifacts left by synthesis models, including unnatural intonation, irregular blinking patterns, or compression anomalies. By combining these signals with behavioral context, AI can flag deepfake calls, video messages, or virtual meetings before they cause harm.

Real-time monitoring is essential for preventing fraud at scale. In financial systems, automated AI models monitor transactions, account activity, and communication streams continuously. Suspicious activity can be blocked instantly, limiting exposure and reducing losses. These systems often operate in layers: initial AI screening identifies potential issues, human analysts review flagged cases, and feedback from investigations is fed back into the AI model to improve future detection. This iterative learning process ensures that the defense keeps pace with adaptive AI attacks.

Cross-platform integration is another key to effective defense. Attackers often move seamlessly between email, messaging apps, social media, and voice calls. Detection systems must correlate signals across multiple channels to detect coordinated attacks. For example, a phishing email followed by a text message requesting confirmation codes may be a single, AI-driven campaign. Integrated monitoring allows organizations to connect the dots, giving a complete view of the attack and enabling more effective responses.

Education and awareness remain foundational to detection. Even the most advanced AI cannot compensate for uninformed or unprepared users. Employees, executives, and individuals must understand common tactics, red flags, and verification protocols. Multi-factor authentication, independent verification of instructions, and established communication procedures all reinforce technical defenses. AI detection systems work best when paired with human awareness, creating a multi-layered security approach that addresses both technological and psychological aspects of fraud.

Finally, collaboration and threat intelligence are crucial. Organizations, banks, law enforcement, and technology providers must share insights about new scams, compromised accounts, and AI attack methods. Machine learning models can be trained on global datasets, improving detection across industries and regions. Threat intelligence platforms allow rapid dissemination of new patterns, helping organizations preempt attacks rather than react after the damage has occurred. In the digital battlefield of AI-driven fraud, collective vigilance multiplies the effectiveness of individual defenses.

In conclusion, detecting AI-powered fraud is a multi-faceted discipline that blends technology, psychology, data science, and human judgment. It requires continuous monitoring, sophisticated analysis, and proactive strategies that evolve alongside the attacks themselves. The combination of machine learning, behavioral analytics, NLP, multimedia forensics, and real-time monitoring provides a powerful defense, but it must be paired with human awareness, structured protocols, and global collaboration. As AI-driven attacks grow more sophisticated, so too must the defenses. Knowledge, preparation, and intelligent systems are the keys to surviving and thriving in a world where deception is automated, scalable, and increasingly invisible.

"The Network That Couldn't Hide"

It started quietly. Small alerts flickered across the dashboards of the security operations center at Aegis Financial, a multinational bank. A few suspicious logins here, an odd wire transfer there, a single phishing email flagged as potentially fraudulent. Nothing that seemed alarming enough to warrant panic. But Maya Patel, the lead AI security analyst, knew better. Something was happening. Something vast, coordinated, and unlike anything she had seen before.

Over the next hours, the incidents escalated. Automated transfers began routing through multiple accounts simultaneously, hundreds at a time. Synthetic identities, created with perfect precision, were attempting to open new lines of credit. AI-generated phishing messages were arriving in employee inboxes, perfectly mimicking the writing style of the CEO, CFO, and even external auditors. The network was alive, learning, and adaptive. Maya could feel it in the way the anomalies were linked, like a machine breathing beneath the surface of the bank's systems.

The team mobilized, layering defenses with AI monitoring, behavioral analysis, and real-time anomaly detection. Alerts cascaded in waves as the system identified logins from improbable locations, micro-transactions in sequences designed to fly under thresholds, and communication patterns that mirrored internal memos but weren't authentic. Maya watched as their AI models cross-referenced every signal: IP addresses, device fingerprints, linguistic markers, transaction flows. Patterns emerged—like the threads of a spiderweb—and she realized they were not chasing individual attacks. They were facing an orchestrated AI fraud network, a digital predator operating at speed and scale no human could match.

The attackers escalated, sending deepfake video calls to the finance team, instructing immediate transfers for "emergency investments." Voices perfectly cloned from prior executive meetings delivered urgent commands. The human operators, trained and alert, hesitated. But Maya's detection system flagged every anomaly—tiny inconsistencies in the speech patterns, subtle timing deviations, and transaction irregularities. The AI monitoring platform blocked the instructions in real time, preventing catastrophic loss.

Over the next 48 hours, the battle intensified. The AI fraud network tried different approaches: manipulating emotional triggers, shifting attack channels, rerouting funds, and sending false verification emails. Maya's team responded by continuously retraining their detection models, using adaptive algorithms to anticipate the attacker's next move. The cyber battlefield became a contest of machine against machine, intelligence against intelligence, with humans orchestrating defenses and interpreting outcomes. Every action the attackers took, every response they tested, became part of the data the defenders used to learn and adapt.

In the end, Aegis Financial survived without significant loss, but the story of "The Network That Couldn't Hide" spread across the industry as a warning. The attackers were never caught—they had vanished as quickly as they had appeared—but the bank's AI detection systems had prevented disaster. Maya reflected on what had happened: the fight was no longer about walls and passwords. It was about intelligence, pattern recognition, psychological insight, and speed. Machines had become both the threat and the shield.

The experience left Maya with a profound understanding of the future of cybersecurity. AI would continue to power attacks that no human could execute alone, but it would also power defenses that no human could achieve without its assistance. In a world where deception was industrialized, survival depended on understanding the mind of the AI, predicting its moves, and building systems capable of outthinking it. "The Network That Couldn't Hide" became a case study, a testament to human ingenuity enhanced by artificial intelligence—a reminder that even in the face of relentless, invisible threats, awareness, preparation, and smart technology could turn the tide.

Chapter 7

AI-Driven Deepfakes and Identity Exploitation

The digital world has entered an era where seeing and hearing no longer guarantee authenticity. Deepfake technology, powered by advanced artificial intelligence, has revolutionized social engineering, phishing, and financial fraud. In the past, scammers relied on emails, phone calls, or fake websites. Today, AI can manipulate audio, video, and images with astonishing realism, allowing criminals to impersonate trusted individuals and orchestrate complex schemes with unparalleled precision. The implications of this technology are profound: trust, once a cornerstone of human interaction, has become a fragile commodity, easily weaponized by machines that can mimic voices, faces, and behaviors flawlessly.

Deepfakes exploit a combination of synthetic media generation and behavioral understanding. AI models analyze video, audio, and text data from publicly available sources—social media, corporate presentations, podcasts, interviews—to create realistic representations of individuals. These models can reproduce a person's facial expressions, gestures, and speech patterns, making video messages indistinguishable from reality. Similarly, voice synthesis technology can clone speech from mere seconds of audio, capturing tone, cadence, accent, and even subtle quirks in pronunciation. When combined, deepfake video and audio create an illusion of authenticity so convincing that even trained professionals can be deceived.

The risks of deepfakes in AI-driven fraud are both personal and organizational. For individuals, a cloned voice or video can be used to extort money, manipulate decisions, or facilitate identity theft. A deepfake call appearing to be from a family member in distress can trigger panic and lead to rapid financial transfer. For organizations, executives can be impersonated in meetings, video calls, or training sessions, enabling fraudulent instructions, data leaks, or unauthorized transactions. Criminals exploit the natural trust humans place in familiar faces and voices, accelerating the success of their attacks.

One of the most powerful aspects of AI deepfakes is adaptability. Machine learning systems analyze responses in real time and adjust their output for maximum effectiveness. If a victim hesitates during a conversation, the system can modify intonation, adjust facial expressions, or introduce new contextual information to reassure or pressure the target. Deepfake campaigns can be deployed at scale, targeting hundreds or thousands of victims simultaneously, each tailored with personalized context to increase compliance.

Unlike traditional scams, these attacks are not static—they evolve and optimize automatically, making each encounter increasingly difficult to resist.

Financial exploitation is a primary goal of deepfake-based attacks. Fraudsters use AI-generated identities to bypass verification systems, authorize transactions, or initiate wire transfers. By combining deepfakes with previously stolen data—such as login credentials, account numbers, or personal details—criminals can simulate authority convincingly and extract funds without physical presence. In high-stakes corporate scenarios, an executive deepfake can authorize a multi-million-dollar transaction in seconds, leaving minimal trace of human involvement and overwhelming traditional oversight mechanisms.

The psychological dimension of deepfake attacks cannot be understated. Humans are wired to trust visual and auditory cues. Seeing a familiar face or hearing a familiar voice triggers automatic trust responses in the brain. AI exploits this instinct, creating compelling illusions that override skepticism. Even cautious, security-conscious individuals can be tricked when confronted with a convincing visual or auditory representation of someone they know. This psychological manipulation is magnified when the deepfake provides additional context: urgent requests, emotional appeals, or insider knowledge that aligns with existing expectations.

Defensive strategies against deepfake exploitation require a combination of technical, procedural, and human-centered approaches. AI-based detection systems analyze digital artifacts, such as inconsistencies in facial movements, unnatural lighting, audio waveform anomalies, and timing discrepancies, to identify synthetic media. Behavioral analytics monitor communication patterns and cross-reference requests with historical norms. Multi-factor authentication, independent verification channels, and structured approval protocols add human oversight that is difficult for AI to bypass. Awareness training ensures that employees and individuals recognize deepfake risks and verify suspicious requests, even when the presentation appears legitimate.

Collaboration is also critical. Threat intelligence sharing between organizations, governments, and technology providers can accelerate detection and mitigate impact. By pooling insights on new deepfake techniques, fraudulent domains, and AI-generated content, stakeholders can improve detection algorithms and educate potential victims. In an environment where deepfake technology evolves daily, collective vigilance and adaptive defenses are essential.

Ultimately, understanding AI-driven deepfakes is about recognizing that digital perception is no longer reliable. Machines can replicate reality with high fidelity, manipulate trust, and exploit psychological vulnerabilities. Protection requires vigilance, layered defenses, and intelligent systems capable of detecting deception in context. Individuals and organizations must adopt a mindset of verification rather than blind trust, recognizing that in the age of AI, authenticity must be continuously validated, not assumed.

"The CEO Who Never Spoke"

It began with a video call that seemed ordinary. Helena Wu, CFO of a mid-sized technology firm, was preparing to approve a critical international transaction when a pop-up appeared: her CEO, Richard Chen, was on the line. The video feed showed him sitting in his office, calm, professional, and entirely familiar. He smiled, nodded toward the camera, and said, "Helena, I need you to authorize this payment immediately. It's urgent for the acquisition." The voice, the face, the gestures—everything matched her memories of countless executive meetings.

Helena hesitated. Something felt slightly off, though she couldn't pinpoint it. Richard's gaze seemed just a fraction too still, his blink pattern slightly inconsistent. Yet the video, the voice, and the context were overwhelmingly convincing. The payment request was consistent with recent discussions and aligned perfectly with the ongoing acquisition. Trust, reinforced by familiarity, pulled her toward compliance. The AI deepfake had created a perfect illusion of authority.

The system behind the video call had analyzed Helena's prior communications. It knew her style of response, her usual work hours, and her decision-making patterns. Every hesitation she expressed triggered subtle changes in the deepfake: pauses became more reassuring, intonation softened, facial micro-expressions conveyed patience and confidence. Helena began typing the account details, believing she was following Richard's explicit instructions. The AI adapted seamlessly, anticipating questions she hadn't even asked yet.

Minutes later, Helena's assistant interrupted with an alert: "I just got an email from Richard's secretary confirming he's out of the country." Panic set in as she realized the video was not real. She tried to end the call, but the deepfake maintained a smooth, lifelike continuity. Her fingers hovered over the send button, the line between reality and simulation blurring. It took the intervention of the IT security team, who had been monitoring for anomalies, to shut down the call and isolate the system. Helena's company narrowly avoided a multi-million-dollar fraud.

The investigation revealed the depth of the attack. Criminals had compiled video clips from public appearances, interviews, and internal meetings, feeding them into an AI model capable of real-time synthesis. Voice samples had been analyzed to clone inflection, tone, and cadence. Contextual information from email threads, schedules, and corporate reports had been used to make the interaction plausible. The AI system had tested Helena's reactions, adapting dynamically to ensure compliance. In seconds, a machine had almost bypassed all human safeguards.

In the aftermath, Helena became a vocal advocate for deepfake awareness and AI verification protocols. The experience underscored that in a world dominated by synthetic media, seeing and hearing are no longer sufficient to confirm authenticity. She implemented multi-layer verification processes, independent approval chains, and AI-powered anomaly detection to safeguard the company against future attacks. Her lesson was clear: trust must be continuously validated, and even the most convincing digital interactions may be elaborate illusions.

The story of "The CEO Who Never Spoke" spread across the industry, a cautionary tale illustrating the power and danger of AI deepfakes. Executives, employees, and individuals alike were forced to confront a new reality: deception had become a precise, adaptive, and almost invisible force. The battle against AI fraud was no longer just about technology—it was about human awareness, critical thinking, and the ability to question the seemingly real. Helena's near-mistake became a turning point, demonstrating that vigilance, preparation, and layered defenses were the only reliable shields against a machine that could impersonate anyone, anywhere, at any time.

Chapter 8

The Future of AI Fraud: Emerging Threats and Strategic Defense

Artificial intelligence continues to evolve at an unprecedented pace, and with that evolution comes a new generation of fraud threats that are faster, smarter, and more adaptive than ever before. The landscape of AI-driven cybercrime is no longer limited to phishing, social engineering, or deepfakes; it now encompasses predictive fraud, autonomous scams, adaptive bots, and attacks that can learn and improve without human intervention. In this emerging environment, understanding the future of AI fraud is critical for individuals, organizations, and governments that aim to protect themselves, their assets, and their digital integrity.

One of the most concerning trends is the rise of **autonomous fraud systems**. Unlike traditional scams that require human oversight, these systems can operate entirely independently. They can monitor networks for vulnerabilities, identify potential victims, generate tailored communication strategies, and execute complex schemes in real time. Autonomous AI fraud systems continuously analyze their own performance, testing different tactics and optimizing their success rates. A single system can simultaneously manage hundreds of campaigns across multiple platforms, including email, SMS, social media, voice calls, and even virtual reality environments, without any direct human involvement.

Predictive fraud is another emerging threat. AI systems can anticipate victim behavior before any action is taken. By analyzing digital footprints, previous interactions, financial behavior, and even psychological tendencies, these systems can calculate the optimal moment to strike. For instance, an AI may detect that a user recently made a large purchase, attended a specific event, or posted certain information online, and then target them with a personalized scam immediately afterward. The predictive nature of these attacks makes traditional reactive defenses almost useless because by the time the fraud is detected, it may already be complete.

Adaptive bot networks are also expanding in sophistication. These networks operate like a decentralized hive, with thousands of bots collaborating in real time, sharing intelligence, and dynamically adjusting their approach based on observed outcomes. If one attack vector fails, the system immediately tests alternatives, reallocates resources, and continues its campaign with optimized precision. These adaptive networks make large-scale fraud campaigns highly resilient and extremely difficult to disrupt, as removing or blocking a single component does little to halt the overall operation.

Deep integration with financial systems is another hallmark of next-generation AI fraud. Criminal AI can interact directly with banking APIs, payment processors, and cryptocurrency networks to automate fund extraction, laundering, and redistribution. Sophisticated systems can also exploit flaws in digital identity verification, bypassing multi-factor authentication, biometric checks, and behavioral analysis. By combining identity manipulation with automated transaction management, AI-driven fraud becomes seamless, fast, and nearly invisible to conventional monitoring systems.

The psychological manipulation inherent in AI scams is also evolving. Advanced AI can now model complex emotional responses, adapting language, tone, and timing to exploit specific vulnerabilities in each target. It can create multi-step interactions that gradually build trust, pressure, and compliance. For example, an AI might first pose as a friendly support agent, then escalate to an authoritative figure, and finally combine urgency and personal context to compel a victim to act. These highly personalized, adaptive strategies are far more effective than traditional scams because they exploit both human behavior and digital context simultaneously. Defense against these emerging threats requires a paradigm shift. Organizations must move from reactive security to **proactive intelligence-driven defense**, leveraging AI for both detection and mitigation. Predictive modeling, anomaly detection, behavioral biometrics, and real-time monitoring become essential tools. Defense systems must be capable of understanding not only individual attacks but also the larger patterns of coordinated AI fraud operations. Integration across platforms and departments, as well as collaboration with external partners and law enforcement, is essential to identify and disrupt networks before they cause damage.

Human awareness continues to be a vital layer of defense. Training, education, and verification protocols must adapt to the changing landscape. Employees, executives, and consumers need to recognize that AI-generated communication—whether text, voice, or video—can be deceptive. Verification through independent channels, procedural redundancies, and cross-checks becomes mandatory. Awareness campaigns must evolve alongside technology, reinforcing the principle that trust cannot be assumed in a digital environment dominated by AI-driven manipulation.

Emerging regulatory frameworks will also play a critical role. Governments and international organizations are beginning to develop laws, standards, and enforcement mechanisms that address AI-driven fraud, deepfake manipulation, and synthetic identity theft. Regulatory compliance will increasingly require organizations to implement robust AI detection, reporting, and mitigation practices. Failure to do so may result not only in financial loss but also in legal and reputational consequences. This regulatory evolution will shape the landscape of AI fraud, influencing both the tactics of attackers and the strategies of defenders.

The future of AI fraud will be characterized by automation, prediction, adaptability, and scale. Threats will continue to evolve faster than traditional human defenses can respond. The key to resilience lies in leveraging AI as both a shield and a sentinel—systems that detect, analyze, and neutralize attacks in real time while empowering humans with awareness and decision-making capability. Organizations and individuals who understand this emerging threat landscape and implement layered, intelligent defenses will be best positioned to survive and thrive in a digital world increasingly dominated by AI deception.

Ultimately, the next generation of AI-driven fraud is not a distant threat; it is already here, silently operating behind screens and within networks. It is adaptive, pervasive, and psychologically sophisticated, challenging the very foundations of trust. By preparing with proactive strategies, AI detection, human vigilance, and regulatory alignment, we can create a future in which fraud is no longer invisible, and in which the intelligent use of technology becomes the ultimate defense against intelligent deception.

"The Phantom Transaction"

Lucas Ramirez, a senior analyst at a major global bank, sat at his workstation late on a Thursday night, reviewing routine transaction logs. Everything appeared normal: payments were processed, accounts balanced, and system alerts minimal. Then a subtle anomaly caught his eye—a transaction sequence that didn't match typical patterns. It was small, almost insignificant, but the precision and timing were unusual. Something deep in Lucas's gut told him to investigate.

Within minutes, his monitoring system flagged a pattern: hundreds of micro-transactions routing through synthetic accounts, each one perfectly timed to avoid triggering alerts. At first, Lucas assumed it was a technical glitch. But as he traced the flow, the picture became horrifyingly clear. An AI-driven fraud network was executing autonomous operations, testing, learning, and optimizing its attack in real time. It was not just a scam; it was a fully orchestrated financial invasion, invisible to conventional monitoring.

The AI system had constructed detailed profiles of hundreds of account holders, combining behavioral data, login histories, and transaction habits. Each synthetic identity acted as a proxy for real-world actors, performing micro-transactions that, when aggregated, moved millions of dollars across multiple financial institutions. The system even adapted its tactics as Lucas's team responded, rerouting funds, adjusting amounts, and exploiting gaps in multi-factor authentication protocols. Every defensive action was anticipated and countered.

Lucas called an emergency response team. Security analysts, AI specialists, and IT engineers scrambled to contain the phantom transaction network. They deployed AI detection models that analyzed behavioral anomalies, monitored account deviations, and flagged inconsistencies in synthetic identity patterns. The system worked tirelessly, mapping the intricate web of fraudulent accounts and tracing the flow of funds back to intermediary cryptocurrency wallets. Each step required careful calibration to prevent triggering retaliatory adaptations from the AI attackers.

As the night wore on, Lucas realized the scale of the threat. The AI network was self-learning, adaptive, and relentless. It did not tire, hesitate, or make mistakes. Every time the team blocked one route, it identified another. The battle was not only technological but psychological; the AI exploited timing, pressure, and expectation to manipulate human defenders, testing their reactions and probing for weaknesses. Hours later, after continuous monitoring and intervention, the team managed to halt the network, freezing the fraudulent transactions before significant funds were lost. Yet the experience left a lingering unease. The attackers had disappeared, leaving no trace of human operators. The system they had fought against had been entirely autonomous, adaptive, and intelligent—a ghost in the financial machine.

"The Phantom Transaction," as Lucas came to call it, became a case study in the emerging era of AI-driven fraud. The bank upgraded its AI monitoring, implemented independent verification protocols, and trained staff to recognize signs of autonomous manipulation. Lucas reflected on the night's events, understanding that in a future dominated by intelligent machines, the line between reality and simulation could be blurred, and vigilance had to extend beyond human perception.

The story spread across the financial industry, highlighting a chilling reality: AI systems could now operate, adapt, and commit fraud on a scale and with a precision impossible for humans alone. But it also demonstrated that with the right combination of AI defense, human oversight, and procedural rigor, even the most advanced autonomous fraud systems could be contained. In a world increasingly dominated by intelligent deception, the fight would continue, and the defenders would have to evolve alongside the machines.

Chapter 9

Legal, Regulatory & Investigative AI Security: Navigating the Rules of the Digital Battlefield

As AI-driven fraud, phishing, and social engineering become increasingly sophisticated, the role of law, regulation, and investigation in cybersecurity is growing more critical. The digital world operates on a foundation of trust, legality, and oversight, yet AI-powered attacks are testing every boundary of existing frameworks. Criminals exploit jurisdictional gaps, loopholes in financial oversight, and the lag between technological innovation and legislative response. Understanding the legal and investigative landscape is essential for organizations, governments, and individuals seeking to protect themselves from AI-driven manipulation, identity theft, and financial crime.

Regulation is one of the primary tools for countering AI fraud. Governments and international organizations are developing frameworks to define what constitutes illegal activity in a digital and AI-driven environment. These regulations address identity theft, financial fraud, phishing, deepfake creation, and synthetic identity operations. Compliance is no longer optional for organizations handling sensitive data, financial transactions, or customer communications. Failure to adhere to these regulations can result in fines, reputational damage, and legal liability, in addition to the direct financial losses caused by AI-driven attacks.

One challenge in this regulatory environment is the global nature of AI crime. Criminal networks often operate across borders, taking advantage of jurisdictions with weaker enforcement or limited cooperation with international law enforcement. AI-driven attacks can originate from anywhere in the world, target victims in multiple countries, and move funds across complex international networks, often through cryptocurrencies or offshore accounts. Regulators are responding by enhancing cross-border cooperation, implementing information-sharing agreements, and harmonizing laws to better address transnational AI fraud.

Investigative techniques have also evolved in response to AI crime. Traditional digital forensics focused on recovering deleted files, tracing IP addresses, and analyzing system logs. Modern AI-driven investigations require advanced analytics, machine learning, and behavioral modeling. Investigators track patterns across multiple platforms, correlate anomalies in network activity, and detect AI-generated content in communications. Deepfake detection, synthetic identity analysis, and predictive modeling have become essential tools for understanding the scope, origin, and methods of AI-driven attacks.

AI itself is now being used in investigations. Machine learning algorithms can parse enormous datasets from financial systems, communications platforms, and social media to identify suspicious activity. Predictive analytics help anticipate fraud before it occurs, while pattern recognition tools reconstruct the flow of stolen funds or compromised data. AI systems can also detect anomalies in language, behavior, or transaction sequences that humans would be unable to analyze at scale. This creates a feedback loop where AI both powers attacks and strengthens investigative capability, leveling the playing field in the digital domain.

Compliance frameworks increasingly require organizations to implement layered security protocols. These may include multi-factor authentication, AI-based anomaly detection, encrypted communication channels, and regular risk assessments. Organizations must also document procedures for identifying, reporting, and responding to AI-driven threats. Regulatory audits often evaluate not only technical controls but also employee training, incident response capabilities, and cross-department coordination. In essence, cybersecurity is no longer only a technical discipline; it is a legal and operational responsibility.

The legal landscape also addresses liability. When AI-generated content or autonomous fraud systems cause harm, courts and regulators are determining who is responsible: the developer, the user, or the deploying organization. Establishing responsibility requires understanding the operational context of AI, the intent of human operators, and the technical autonomy of systems. This evolving area of law highlights the importance of accountability, governance, and ethical design in AI systems. Organizations that fail to implement robust governance risk being implicated even when attacks are technically carried out by AI.

Education and awareness complement legal and technical defenses. Employees, executives, and consumers must understand both the threats posed by AI and the regulatory requirements surrounding data handling, financial transactions, and digital communications. Effective training programs include not only technical protocols but also guidance on recognizing manipulative tactics, reporting suspicious activity, and verifying requests independently. A well-informed human layer, combined with AI detection and regulatory compliance, forms the most resilient defense against AI-driven crime. Finally, collaboration is paramount.

Law enforcement agencies, technology companies, financial institutions, and cybersecurity firms must share intelligence, report emerging AI threats, and coordinate investigations. The complexity and scale of AI-driven fraud make isolation ineffective; the only effective approach is a combined, intelligence-driven, multi-jurisdictional response. By combining legal oversight, investigative technology, human vigilance, and cross-organizational collaboration, society can mitigate the risks of AI-driven fraud while preparing for future threats.

Understanding the intersection of AI, law, and digital investigation is crucial for survival in today's cyber environment. Regulatory compliance, proactive detection, cross-border collaboration, and ethical governance are no longer optional; they are integral components of resilience. The threats posed by AI-driven crime are not static, and neither can defenses be. Organizations, individuals, and governments must operate with agility, intelligence, and foresight to protect trust, financial stability, and digital integrity in an age where deception is automated and pervasive.

"The Investigator Who Followed the Ghosts"

Detective Elena Morales sat in a small office cluttered with monitors, servers, and digital logs. The case before her was unlike anything she had faced: millions of dollars disappeared from global accounts, leaving barely a trace, and victims were reporting interactions with machines they could not see. The AI fraud network she was investigating had no physical presence. It existed in servers, code, and algorithmic decision-making. To her team, it felt like chasing ghosts.

The first breakthrough came when Elena noticed subtle correlations in transaction logs. Accounts that appeared unrelated shared timing patterns, similar routing paths, and behavioral markers too precise to be random. She realized she was looking at an AI-driven system capable of coordinating hundreds of micro-fraud operations simultaneously. Each transaction, each interaction, was a strand in a larger web that the network had spun with incredible sophistication.

Elena's investigation relied heavily on AI-assisted analytics. Machine learning models were trained to detect patterns of synthetic identity creation, analyze transaction anomalies, and flag irregular communications. The AI investigators themselves identified deepfakes in video calls, inconsistencies in voice patterns, and subtle deviations in language. The machines were not only used to commit the crime—they were essential in unraveling it. Elena often marveled at the irony: AI fighting AI in a digital battle invisible to the human eye.

As the case progressed, Elena tracked the network across international borders. Servers in Europe, cryptocurrency wallets in Asia, and compromised accounts in North America all formed a sprawling, interconnected system. The criminals had exploited jurisdictional gaps, knowing law enforcement coordination lagged behind. Elena had to work with foreign agencies, technology companies, and financial institutions to piece together the full scope. The investigation became a complex puzzle of real-time collaboration and advanced analytics.

One of the most challenging moments occurred when the network began using adaptive strategies. As investigators traced one series of transactions, the AI redirected funds, created new synthetic identities, and rerouted communications. Every countermeasure was anticipated. It was like playing chess against a master who could think thousands of moves ahead in seconds. Elena's team had to innovate constantly, deploying predictive algorithms, anomaly detection, and pattern recognition to keep up with a moving, evolving adversary.

Human factors also played a role. Employees and account holders were being manipulated by deepfake calls, AI-generated emails, and targeted social engineering. Elena had to coordinate awareness campaigns, train staff on verification procedures, and ensure independent approvals for transactions. These human-centered interventions worked alongside AI monitoring, forming a layered defense that gradually began to contain the threat. It became clear that technology alone was not enough—vigilance, education, and process integrity were essential.

Finally, after weeks of tireless investigation, Elena's team managed to isolate a critical segment of the network: a cluster of synthetic identities funneling millions through offshore cryptocurrency wallets. By coordinating with financial regulators and using AI detection systems to trace and freeze assets, they prevented further losses. Though the network's operators were not immediately identified, the impact of the containment was significant. The ghostly AI system had been disrupted, if only temporarily, and millions of dollars were safeguarded.

"The Investigator Who Followed the Ghosts" became a case study in AI-driven fraud investigation. It highlighted the challenges of prosecuting and defending against autonomous, intelligent systems and emphasized the need for collaboration, advanced analytics, and human vigilance. Elena reflected that the digital battlefield was no longer defined by physical evidence or human operators alone—it was a constantly evolving landscape of intelligent machines, psychological manipulation, and financial automation. Surviving in this world required not only technology but foresight, strategy, and an unrelenting commitment to understanding the invisible adversaries operating just beyond the human senses.

Chapter 10

The Future of AI Cybersecurity: Autonomous Defense and Digital Resilience

As artificial intelligence continues to advance, the battleground of cybersecurity is evolving into a contest of autonomous systems versus autonomous threats. AI-powered fraud, phishing, social engineering, deepfakes, and synthetic identity attacks are no longer isolated incidents—they are components of complex, adaptive networks capable of learning, optimizing, and exploiting human and technical vulnerabilities simultaneously. The imperative for organizations, governments, and individuals is clear: defenses must also be intelligent, adaptive, and proactive. The future of AI cybersecurity lies in the integration of autonomous defense mechanisms, predictive threat modeling, and resilient operational strategies that can respond to unseen threats in real time.

Autonomous defense systems are at the forefront of this evolution. Unlike traditional firewalls or signature-based antivirus programs, these systems continuously analyze incoming data, detect anomalies, and respond without waiting for human input. Machine learning models process vast amounts of communication, transaction, and behavioral data to identify potential threats, from subtle deviations in email syntax to irregularities in financial flows. When an anomaly is detected, these systems can automatically isolate compromised accounts, block suspicious transactions, and quarantine potential malware, minimizing damage before it spreads.

Predictive AI modeling is another critical component of future cybersecurity. By analyzing patterns from historical attacks, AI can anticipate emerging threats and prepare defenses preemptively. This includes forecasting the likelihood of phishing attempts, predicting which individuals may be targeted by social engineering, and identifying networks at risk of intrusion. Predictive models also consider psychological patterns, such as susceptibility to manipulation, enabling organizations to implement preemptive safeguards like additional verification steps, alerts, or mandatory training interventions.

Behavioral biometrics and continuous authentication are essential tools in autonomous defense. AI systems can monitor typing patterns, mouse movements, device usage, and even network behavior to create a digital profile for each user. Any deviation from expected patterns can trigger alerts or automatically lock sensitive systems. These techniques protect against account takeovers, synthetic identity attacks, and credential-based fraud. By focusing on human behavior rather than just static credentials, cybersecurity shifts from reactive to proactive defense, making it harder for AI-driven attackers to succeed.

AI deepfake detection is increasingly important in this landscape. Advanced forensic algorithms analyze subtle inconsistencies in audio, video, and images to detect synthetic media. Techniques such as facial micro-expression analysis, voice waveform irregularities, and contextual cross-verification allow AI systems to identify impersonations in real time. These tools are deployed in corporate communications, financial approvals, and remote collaboration platforms to ensure that any request for sensitive action is authentic. In an environment where seeing and hearing no longer guarantees truth, these detection systems become a vital first line of defense.

Collaboration and information sharing are critical elements of future AI cybersecurity. Autonomous defense systems function optimally when they can exchange intelligence across platforms, organizations, and geographies. Threat intelligence networks enable rapid dissemination of newly discovered attack vectors, compromised domains, and AI tactics. By pooling data and insights, defenders can preemptively strengthen their systems against attacks that are already underway elsewhere. This collective approach is vital in combating AI-driven threats, which often operate globally and adapt faster than any single organization can respond.

Human awareness remains a cornerstone of cybersecurity, even in an era of autonomous defense. Technology alone cannot prevent manipulation or error. Employees, executives, and individuals must be trained to recognize suspicious communications, verify critical requests, and apply verification procedures consistently. Autonomous systems amplify human decision-making, but vigilance and critical thinking are still essential to close gaps that AI alone cannot monitor, particularly in scenarios involving social engineering or deepfake interactions.

Regulatory compliance is evolving alongside AI-driven threats. Governments are developing rules and standards for AI security, requiring organizations to implement both technical defenses and procedural safeguards. Compliance audits now include assessments of AI detection capabilities, threat response protocols, and human oversight mechanisms. Legal frameworks are adapting to hold organizations accountable for lapses in autonomous defenses, emphasizing that resilience is not optional but mandatory in a world dominated by intelligent, adaptive cyber threats. The future of AI cybersecurity emphasizes resilience. Systems must be designed not only to prevent attacks but to survive and adapt when breaches occur. This involves layered defenses, automated incident response, continuous monitoring, and rapid recovery strategies. By combining predictive modeling, autonomous interventions, behavioral analytics, and human oversight, organizations can achieve digital resilience that protects both assets and trust. In an environment where AI can create, manipulate, and deceive at scale, the ability to detect, respond, and adapt in real time will define survival.

Ultimately, AI cybersecurity is no longer just a technical problem; it is a strategic, operational, and ethical challenge. The threats are intelligent, adaptive, and relentless, requiring an equally sophisticated approach. Organizations and individuals must embrace autonomous defense, continuous learning, and collaboration to thrive in the digital landscape. Knowledge, vigilance, and intelligent systems together form the foundation for enduring digital security in an era where deception is automated and nearly invisible.

"The Day the Network Fought Back"

It began as a normal Tuesday morning at Centurion Financial Services. Analysts monitored transactions, emails flowed, and routine systems checks proceeded as usual. Then the first anomaly appeared: a cluster of suspicious transactions, small amounts, routed through newly created accounts. At first, no one paid it much attention, assuming it was an error. But Cassandra Li, the lead AI security officer, immediately recognized a pattern reminiscent of prior AI-driven attacks she had studied. The network was under assault.

By mid-morning, the attack escalated. AI-generated phishing emails targeted executives, while automated bots attempted to bypass login systems and initiate unauthorized transfers. Deepfake video calls simulated senior management, instructing employees to approve urgent payments. The sophistication was alarming: every message, every transaction, every interaction was precisely tailored to human psychology and corporate procedures. This was not random fraud; it was an intelligent, adaptive adversary operating across multiple channels simultaneously.

Cassandra's autonomous defense system sprang into action. Real-time behavioral analytics detected anomalies in typing patterns, login locations, and transaction timing. Machine learning models analyzed incoming messages for linguistic and structural inconsistencies, identifying AI-generated content with high confidence. Automated scripts blocked suspicious transactions, quarantined compromised accounts, and issued alerts to human operators. For the first time, the network itself seemed to fight back in a synchronized, intelligent response. The attackers adapted, testing different approaches, rerouting funds, and adjusting phishing messages to bypass detection. But the autonomous defense systems were equally adaptive. Predictive algorithms anticipated next steps based on historical patterns and behavioral analysis, creating dynamic countermeasures in real time. Cassandra and her team monitored the operations closely, intervening when necessary but relying primarily on AI systems to manage the complexity and speed of the attack.

By afternoon, the battle had reached a critical juncture. Deepfake calls targeted the finance department, simulating urgent instructions from the CEO. Employees hesitated, confused by the realism of the messages. Cassandra instructed the system to deploy cross-verification protocols, automatically alerting staff to verify instructions through multiple channels. The AI system analyzed responses, flagging discrepancies and blocking high-risk actions before any funds could move. Slowly, the tide began to turn—the attackers' adaptive strategies were being neutralized.

Hours of intense monitoring, real-time response, and AI-human collaboration culminated in containment. The network had identified and isolated the malicious accounts, blocked all active threats, and traced the flows of attempted fraudulent transactions to the originating systems. For Cassandra, it was both relief and awe. The attackers had been sophisticated, but the integrated AI defense, predictive modeling, and procedural rigor had prevailed. Centurion Financial Services had survived an unprecedented, fully autonomous AI attack.

The aftermath was sobering. The attackers had vanished, leaving no human operators in sight. The AI system had tested human trust, psychological response, and procedural gaps, exploiting weaknesses with precision. Yet the defense network had adapted, learned, and responded faster than the attackers anticipated. Cassandra documented the case extensively, calling it "The Day the Network Fought Back," highlighting the lessons learned: autonomous defense, continuous monitoring, human oversight, and procedural rigor were essential in a world where intelligent threats operated invisibly, globally, and relentlessly.

The story spread across the industry, emphasizing a fundamental truth: in the age of AI, cybersecurity is a living, adaptive discipline. Machines are both the threat and the shield, capable of deception, manipulation, and exploitation—but also capable of detection, mitigation, and defense. Organizations that embraced autonomous systems, predictive analytics, and integrated human oversight would survive; those that relied solely on traditional methods would fall victim to intelligent, adaptive adversaries. Cassandra's experience became a blueprint for resilience in an era where AI no longer just threatens—it challenges the very foundations of trust, decision-making, and human judgment in the digital realm.

Final Thoughts

As we conclude this journey through the intricate world of AI-driven phishing, social engineering, and fraud, it is clear that the landscape of cybersecurity has fundamentally changed. The threats we face are no longer static or isolated—they are adaptive, intelligent, and scalable. Criminal networks now leverage artificial intelligence to manipulate human behavior, replicate trusted identities, and execute financial crimes with unprecedented speed and precision. What once relied on human intuition, charm, and deception can now be automated, analyzed, and optimized continuously. Understanding these developments is not just a professional necessity; it is a personal imperative. Everyone interacting with the digital world is potentially vulnerable, and awareness is the first line of defense.

AI-powered attacks have demonstrated that the most significant vulnerabilities lie not in technology but in human psychology. Trust, authority, urgency, fear, curiosity, and empathy are exploited with a precision no traditional security system could counter alone. Every phishing email, social engineering campaign, deepfake call, or synthetic identity attack is designed to exploit the predictable ways humans respond under pressure. Recognizing these vulnerabilities allows individuals and organizations to implement checks, balances, and verification methods that disrupt the attacker's advantage. Awareness, vigilance, and critical thinking are the human components of cybersecurity that no AI can replicate—yet these are precisely what attackers seek to bypass.

Defending against AI-driven fraud requires a multifaceted strategy that blends technology, education, and governance. Advanced detection systems, powered by AI themselves, can monitor for anomalous behavior, analyze transactional patterns, and identify suspicious communication in real time. Behavioral biometrics, deepfake detection, anomaly monitoring, and predictive analytics form the backbone of modern defense mechanisms. These systems work best when integrated with human oversight, structured procedural controls, and continuous training. Defense is not a single tool or software—it is an ecosystem, a layered approach combining human intuition with machine precision.

Education remains a critical pillar of cybersecurity resilience. Employees, executives, and individual users must be trained to recognize potential scams, validate unusual requests, and understand the methods AI fraud systems employ. Simulated attacks, interactive training modules, and awareness campaigns help reinforce the habits necessary to prevent breaches. Knowledge empowers individuals to act as an active layer of defense, questioning suspicious communications rather than responding reflexively. Awareness and preparedness dramatically reduce the effectiveness of AI-driven manipulation.

Legal and regulatory frameworks are evolving to meet these new challenges. Governments are establishing laws to address synthetic identities, deepfake fraud, AI-generated phishing, and autonomous scams. Organizations are increasingly accountable not only for breaches but for their preparedness, governance, and response strategies. Compliance audits now evaluate technical defenses, training programs, and procedural rigor. Understanding the legal landscape is vital for organizations to navigate liability, protect assets, and maintain trust with clients, customers, and stakeholders.

Cross-industry collaboration is also essential. AI-driven threats are global and adaptive; they cross borders, platforms, and industries with ease. Sharing intelligence, coordinating responses, and analyzing patterns across organizations and sectors strengthen defenses and reduce the impact of attacks. Threat intelligence networks allow real-time sharing of information about emerging scams, compromised accounts, and sophisticated AI attack methods. In this interconnected digital ecosystem, no single entity can defend itself in isolation. Looking forward, the future of cybersecurity will be defined by adaptation. AI-driven threats will continue to grow more intelligent, faster, and more sophisticated. Organizations and individuals must adopt a mindset of continuous vigilance, ongoing learning, and proactive defense. Technology alone cannot solve the problem; it must be paired with human awareness, layered processes, and collaboration. The battle for digital security will always be a contest between intelligent systems—both malicious and protective—operating in parallel with human oversight.

Ultimately, the key lesson is that trust is a finite resource in the digital age, and protecting it requires knowledge, preparation, and adaptability. AI can create, manipulate, and exploit human perception, but it cannot replace informed decision-making, procedural rigor, or ethical governance. By understanding the threats, implementing layered defenses, and continuously training humans to recognize and respond to deception, individuals and organizations can create resilient systems capable of surviving and thriving in an environment dominated by intelligent cyber threats.

As you close this book, remember: the digital world is no longer merely a tool; it is a dynamic environment where deception is automated and pervasive. The strategies, tools, and insights presented here are designed to equip you with the knowledge and methods to defend against AI-driven fraud, phishing, social engineering, and deepfake attacks. Vigilance, preparation, and intelligent systems are the keys to safeguarding both assets and trust in the age of artificial intelligence.

www.ingramcontent.com/pod-product-compliance
Ingram Content Group UK Ltd.
Pitfield, Milton Keynes, MK11 3LW, UK
UKHW020157290926
15471UKWH00005B/925

9 798295 598470